*To Cindy
Best Wishes &
Happy Writing
Lynn Bradley
6-18-94*

THE
INCIDENTAL &
PERTINENT
STUFF

FOR BEGINNING

FICTION WRITERS

written and illustrated

by Lynn Bradley

ISBN 0-9637150-0-3

Published by Talent by the Lb.
P O Box 531, Sugar Land, TX 77487

HOW YOU BEGIN

Study the craft
Of writing a draft
Write for awhile
Develop a style
Rewrite it twice
Make it look nice
Rewrite it again
And now you begin

"... and see if you can get a few more of them published."

CONTENTS

INTRODUCTION

The purpose of this book is to help beginning writers in their initial search for the information, techniques and procedures necessary to start on the road toward publication. It is not comprehensive. It is not all a writer needs to know. However, I believe that if you learn these basics, you will be able to develop your wonderful creativity into a marketable product.

The information in TIPS for Beginning Fiction Writers, was gathered from many sources: Creative Writing class under Michael Sofranko at Houston Community College, Screenwriting under Sam Havens at Rice University Continuing Education, quite a few workshops and seminars and many hours of reading. I encourage you to take classes, attend workshops, seminars and conferences--and learn the craft of writing.

Except for the basic instincts we have at birth, everything has to be learned. When we first try to talk, we jabber. When we first try to walk, we fall. Each job, each social skill has to be learned.

Creative writing comes to some of us through stories in our heads. No matter how great our creativity, until we put those stories on paper (or disk), they can't be sold. We have to learn what editors are looking for, what will sell. We have to learn how to structure, develop, prepare and present our creativity.

Every business, every area of life has its own jargon. From "sit-upon" to "four and float," only those involved in the applicable arena understand the specialized language.

Writing, too, has its own jargon. Many of the words that are common to experienced writers have only a vague meaning to the beginner if they hold any meaning at all. For this reason, I am starting with a simple vocabulary list. By studying and referring to this list, the rest of the information will be more easily understood. As for the rest of the book, it is in no particular order. I would encourage you to pick and choose as the Muse strikes.

Of course, there are many relevant words which have been omitted, but please remember, this is for beginners. I would suggest you begin a notebook or data file of particular bits of writing advice that help you along your way. Writing, or entering, each bit of new (for you) information reinforces your leaning and helps it become a working part of your writing. The idea is for these tips and bits to become automatically included when you write.

Keep reading. . . and keep writing.

Lynn Bradley
(Forever a beginner)

VOCABULARY

Plot - A sequence of events that leads from an established problem through obstacles to a conclusion.

Protagonist - Main character (whether we like him/her or not). He must be someone or something the reader can sympathize with and care about the outcome of his/her/its life. The reader must want Character to "win" whether he does or not.

Antagonist - Person, place, circumstance or thing in opposition to protagonist. The bad guy or bad circumstance to be overcome. A story is only as strong as its antagonist.

Characterization - Information given about each character; details of description, behavior and motivation to make them seem real to the reader. The protagonist is usually developed more fully than other characters.

Stock Characters - Also called Cardboard Characters. These are the fringe characters that don't have to be rounded out or developed unless they become important in the story. For example: The doctor, his white lab coat flapping, said, ". . ." No more details about the man are needed if his only purpose is to get information to the reader once or twice.

Irony - The equation between two events where one part mocks the other. Verbal irony is when a character says one thing and the reader knows the opposite is true. For example, the town drunk says, "I never touch the stuff."

Setting - The context within which the action takes place. This is not confined to geography, but also includes the time of year, mood (hostile, friendly, romantic) and condition (rich, poor, common).

Pacing - The rate at which a plot unfolds. Slow pacing is usually accomplished by using longer sentences and no dialogue. To move it along faster, shorten sentences, add dialogue. For punch, (once, or at most twice in a short story) add a two or three word sentence at the end of a paragraph. Even a fast-moving plot needs slow sections to build tension, give the reader a breather and develop the characters. Alternate pace.

Imagery - Showing the reader by being specific. Don't say night creature, use armadillo or skunk. Draw pictures with concrete nouns and active verbs.

Details - Must be selective. All details are not needed, but all important ones are.

Weight - As applied to sentences. Regardless of length, all sentences carry equal weight; therefore, short sentences have more power than long ones. Do not overpower a story with short sentences or it will be choppy.

POV - Point of View - May refer to Narrator's (not necessarily Author's) point of view or Character's "attitude" toward life.

OMNISCIENT POV - (om ni' shent) - Told in third person. Narrator can go anywhere, including into minds of all characters.

LIMITED OMNISCIENT POV - Told in third person, but stays with one character and goes into only mind of that character. (This POV most closely approximates real life.

FIRST PERSON POV - Author is inside, or becomes, one character.

OBJECTIVE POV - Usually nonfiction. Author can't go into minds or emotions, merely evaluates or interprets what is visual.

Novel - A long story. Must be a specific story, no matter how intricate; usually covers a longer time span and has more fully developed characters than a short story.

Formula story - Can be a novel or short story. Usually, boy meets girl, etc.

Genre - Also Category Novels. Any book that can be put in a particular slot: mystery, romance, adventure, western, historical, is a genre novel.

Mainstream - Any novel that doesn't fit a category or genre. Usually more fully developed characters and plot.

Elements of Fiction - Conflict, crisis, resolution. Only trouble is interesting. The struggle is the story!

Drama - Desire plus danger. Central character must have burning desire and dangerous obstacle.

Description - Specific, concrete "word pictures."

HOW YOU BEGIN

Study the craft
Of writing a draft
Write for awhile
Develop a style
Rewrite it twice
Make it look nice
Rewrite it again
And now you begin

BEFORE THE BEGINNING

All writing should contain these five elements. The writer should be able to identify them prior to each project.

1) **Purpose.** Is your goal to convince, entertain or inform?

2) **Audience.** Who is the piece written for? Who would buy it?

3) **Thesis.** What is the main point? Primary conflict? Resolution?

4) **Tone.** What is the attitude of the speaker (Narrator) toward the subject?

5) **Strategy.** What method will be used to disclose the information until plot is unfolded and conflict resolved?

Each story must be about conflict, but there are only SIX (6) conflicts:

MAN vs MAN (OR WOMAN)
MAN vs NATURE (ELEMENTS OR ANIMALS)
MAN vs SOCIETY
MAN vs MACHINE (OR ALIEN)
MAN vs GOD
MAN vs HIMSELF

KNOW YOUR CHARACTERS

Develop a personal history on all main characters. Put it in a notebook somewhere, but not in the story or script. Bits may be dropped into the storyline as needed, but usually most will not be necessary. What this will do is give you the information you need to know how your characters will act in any given situation. Depending on the type of work you are writing, you may want to go back as many as six generations. For most genre novels, parents and grandparents do help firm up a character's past and determine present actions, but beyond that I'm not sure any in-depth study needs to be done. On an historical saga, however, we need to know whereof we speak.

Avoid "sit-down scenes" where one character fills in another on his personal history unless the scene is wrapped in a "frame of tension," i.e., a pair is telling war stories while they wait for a possibly terrible event.

One way to know your character is to write a first-person story in that character's persona. I usually begin with, "Hi, my name is Character. I was born _____ and grew up feeling. . .. I remember. . .." I go into early jobs, school, first boyfriend, siblings, fears, etc. By the time I start the book, I know whose story it is and how my character feels about herself and her life.

Another method uses the following chart. It is self-explanatory. I got this as a handout at a writers' seminar at Alvin Community College in Alvin, Texas, from historical romance writer Vivian Vaughn. I've modified it to include other traits that have been helpful for me.

Sometimes I fill in the blanks after I've written the first person narrative; sometimes I use only the form. Whichever way you get to know your characters is the best way for you, but remember--you need to know a lot more about the people in your fictional world than any reader does or your characters will not be believable.

Whadda ya mean, get a real job? I'm a writer!

DEVELOP
STRONG CHARACTERS

Your central or main character, the protagonist, makes the story happen. He or she makes choices that effect herself, other characters and the outcome of the story. The struggle of the protagonist is the story. He must be strong, vivid and your reader must care what happens to him. Here are some of the ways in which this can be accomplished.

First, establish Character's need or desire and why he can't have it. Character must have a burning desire for an acceptable reward--love, homestead, health or acceptance of disability, music career, acting career. What is keeping him from it and what he does to overcome this obstacle--that is your story and where his strength must be directed.

Show Character's physical description. Make your protagonist unique physically. It doesn't have to be a limp or a twitchy eye. Nervous habits like rubbing bangs out of her eyes, pushing his glasses up on his nose--anything that helps your reader develop a mental picture. It is the "mind-movies" that make reading so special.

Don't forget to do wardrobe. How Character dresses tells the reader something about him or her. For minor characters, sometimes you will only need clothing to identify the speaker, (With his lab coat flapping behind him, . . .). Or you may want to use wardrobe to show your protagonist is "out of character" in the current scene. (Jason had never worn a tuxedo, but he had a feeling this wouldn't be his last night in formal attire.)

Know Character's point of view (attitude toward life-- not to be confused with Narrator's POV). Does your character wake up singing or growling? Is his/her basic instinct to trust people? Or not? What are Character's favorite situations? Dancing? Picnics? Sports events? Does he think the world is in a hopeless state? Does he believe money cures all ills? Your character's general attitude toward himself and others motivates his actions. If you know your character at depth, you'll know what that character's reaction will be in every situation.

Develop obstacles for Character to overcome (or not) as he struggles to reach his desparate need or burning desire. Never use coincidence or weather to solve a problem, but they can be useful for making his situation worse, giving him more to overcome. And each difficulty overcome brings admiration from your reader.

Give Character his own voice and particular way of phrasing through using special word choices or repeated phrases. A reader can know Character's level of education and tone through speech patterns. There's a big difference in characterization between, "I say, I could do with a spot of ale" and "Say, Buddy, gimme a beer" or "Gosh, Honey, do you think we could stop gardening long enough for a beer."

Make Character able to solve a problem or have an understanding by the end of the book that was impossible in the beginning. This gives importance to the work and satisfaction to the reader. Always show how Character's suffering proves her worthiness for a satisfying, rewarding conclusion. Your readers will love you and your character.

CHARACTER DEVELOPMENT CHART

STORY: _____

_____

_____

_____

MAIN CHARACTER: _____

_____

PHYSICAL DESCRIPTION: _____

_____

_____

_____

PERSONAL BACKGROUND: _____

_____

_____

_____

CHARACTER TRAITS: (3 POSITIVE AND 3 NEGATIVE)
1. _____
2. _____
3. _____

1. _____
2. _____
3. _____

CHARACTER TAGS:
1. (APPEARANCE) _____

_____

2. (SPEECH) _____

3. (MANNERISMS)_____

CHARACTER'S GREATEST FEAR: _____
_____
_____

GREATEST DESIRE:_____
_____
_____

SELF-CONCEPT: _____
_____

POV/HOW REACTS TO WORLD & LIFE IN GENERAL:
_____
_____
_____
_____

FAVORITE ENVIRONMENT: _____
_____
_____

EXPERIENCE/SKILLS: _____
_____
_____
_____

12_____

IDEALS: _____

_____
_____

ARC: (ESTABLISH PROBLEM, PROTAGONIST GETS
NEW INFO, DECISION, ALL IS LOST, SUPREME
EFFORT, CLIMAX, CHARACTER CHANGE)

_____
_____
_____
_____
_____
_____
_____
_____
_____
_____
_____
_____
_____
_____
_____
_____
_____
_____
_____
_____
_____
_____

THE CHARACTERIZATION OF
CENTRAL CHARACTER

The following information on building characters was taken from a course in screenwriting. Most of what I learned there readily applies to novel writing.

The **central character** is the one who makes the story happen. He makes choices that affect himself and other characters and the outcome of the story. He must have a **burning hunger** that makes the story happen.

NEED + DESIRE = MOTIVATION

The driving force of a story is the central character's need--his need to get, keep, win, have, etc. He must have great willpower to get the job done or do whatever is necessary to get what he wants.

Make the central character want something, then don't let him have it--until the end. The central character should demonstrate that perseverance pays off. He develops a plan of action, usually dangerous (physically or emotionally) and/or unlikely and makes a gutsy decision. (Remember Elliot saying, "I'm gonna keep him" about E.T.?) The results of Character's decisions changes him. This change is sometimes called an "ARC."

ARC is the growth of a character from the opening point to the end. From A to Z. This is shown in a change of attitude of the character and a change of action. This is one measure of a story. (Remember when Rod Steiger carries Sidney Poitier's suitcase at the end of the movie In the Heat of the Night?

We must make the audience (reader) care about the central character. We do this by showing his burning desire, then not letting him have it.

THE STRUGGLE IS THE STORY!

THERE ARE **THREE P's** to consider when developing a well-rounded character.

Profession

Personal

Private

As a writer, you should be clear on each of these P's for each of your primary characters whether or not all the information you know is used or not. Show a character's profession by describing the sign on his door, his dialogue, the clothes he wears (lab coat or overalls tell us a lot about a character's profession, though they alone do not pinpoint it).

Show his personal relationship with others in dialogue and action.

His private thoughts show in what he thinks and does when he is alone. This can be shown in letters, thoughts and actions that take place when Character is alone. A good illustration of this third P is illustrated when a Goody Two-shoes type tells a retarded boy to take a carrot to his wife. When the wife says, "Why did you tell him a carrot?" he denies it and says he told the boy a candle, which is what his wife requested. This lets the reader know what a jerk he is by revealing his private self.

TAG, YOU'RE IT!

A tag is a characteristic that sets one character apart from another. There are several ways to "tag" characters in either their voice, dress or physical attributes, emotions or attitudes.

Tag each character's voice by giving him or her a special speech pattern, vocabulary, grammar, word choice and repeated words. The reader should be able to recognize a character by the dialogue.

Give each character a physical tag: short, tall, blond, swarthy, in a wheelchair, one arm missing (Remember The Fugitive?), old, young.

A bubbly personality, a sourpuss, a sad or happy character is an emotional tag. Of course, emotions change, but basic characteristics don't. The basics make characters memorable. Use anything believable that sets Character apart.

NO HAYSTACK HERE

Where are the words
That draw the pictures
And tell the reader the news?
They're fast asleep
Recouping their strength
And waiting to hear from my Muse.

THE BIG QUESTIONS

Before I start a story, there are several questions I must answer to have any idea where my story is going. These questions can also be applied to the completed novel (the book), and very effectively to each scene. The questions are:

WHY? WHO? WHERE? WHEN? WHAT?

THE BIG DECISION?

THE BOOK:
WHY am I writing this story? Is it to entertain, inform, persuade?

WHO is my audience? Who will buy it?

WHERE will I market this story?

WHEN will I finish this manuscript?

WHAT category or genre does it fit?

DECISION? Is this the next book I need/want to write?

THE STORY:
WHY is my main character interesting?

WHO is my main character?

WHERE does the story take place?

WHEN does the story take place?

WHAT is the story about?

DECISION? What is the main character's choice of action to solve the problem that either makes the problem worse or creates one or resolves the story?

THE SCENE:

WHY am I writing this scene? To further the story? Build the character? Show conflict?

WHO is the main character in this scene? Who is Character interacting with?

WHERE is this scene set?

WHEN does this scene take place?

WHAT happens in this scene to further the story?

DECISION? Who makes what decision in this scene that changes the relationship of the characters.

STILL SEEKING

The perfect place
Is what I crave
To write in peace
And solitude

Till it is found
I'll have to write
In every stolen
Interlude

CENTRAL CASTING
(YOUR PROTAGONIST)

Your central or main character makes the story happen. He or she makes choices that effect herself, other characters and the outcome of the story. The struggle is the story.

To develop strong characters:

Establish and be aware of Character's need. Character should need whatever desperately.

Show Character's physical description. Make each character unique physically.

Pay attention to showing what characters are wearing. How they dress tells the reader something about them.

Know each character's point of view (attitude toward life - not to be confused with Narrator's POV).

Develop obstacles for Character to overcome (or not) as he struggles to meet need or burning desire.

Know your character's three Ps: Professional life, Personal life and Private life.

Give each character his own voice and particular way of phrasing, special word choices or repeated phrases. Know and show Character's level of education and tone.

Make characters realistic, but still a bit larger than life-- and always flawed.

Use strong motivation to take Protagonist from victim to hero status. Never use "knowing intuitively" as a solution. At maximum strain (all-is-lost point), hero has to do something to triumph, i.e., make a difficult choice, overthrow evil, leave homeland.

Always show how Character's suffering proves her worthiness for satisfying, rewarding conclusion.

TRY TO WRITE WITH...

consistent narrator's tone and level of vocabulary;
variety of sentence structure and length;
variety of word choices;
strong active verbs;
alternating dialogue and narrative;
"page-turner" chapter endings;
good smooth transitions;
sharp, concise dialogue.

"No, I don't think it's another Western."

FROM HERE TO THERE

Transitions--that tricky way of getting a character into the next morning or the next town. It is often done best with a named emotion, the weather or time of day.

EXAMPLES:

It was still raining as he. . .

The sadness was still with her when she opened her eyes the next morning.

(It began raining in the previous scene.) Three days of steady rain had changed nothing.

By morning, her anger had cooled.

Here is an alternate method of transition that can also be used when changing POV character, skipping chunks of time or distance: insert an extra line, add

* * *

to let the reader know that time, space or character has changed.

* * *

Be a penguin when you write: Go with the floe.

HOW BIG IS IT?

How big is a ball? How green is a lizard? How do you show without telling?

Inadequate description prevents a reader from "seeing" your story. Too much description leaves the poor reader with nothing to feed his imagination. Getting the description vivid without overdoing is your goal. But how do you show how big, small, blue, shiny, beautiful or ugly anything is without resorting to a list of adjectives? Think similies and metaphors.

Similies can make description specific and use most of the senses: sight, hearing, touch, taste and smell. Generally, similies use the word like or as. Vague, generic terms are like mush. Strong description is like oatmeal and brown sugar. These two similies illustrate the importance of being specific. Inspite of using the similie "like mush," a rather indefinite picture comes to mind; whereas, "oatmeal and brown sugar" conjurs up texture, aroma, color and taste. With similies, as with any scene, being specific is the difference between showing and telling. Always strive to "show" your readers, but please, avoid the overused, oh-so-familiar similies: mad as a wet hornet, gentle as a dove, high as a kite, old as Methusela, playful as a kitten. . . you get the idea.

With metaphors, be careful not to mix them up. Or, if you do, make it deliberately humorous. "The man was a bull going in for the kill. His mighty branches whipped toward his adversary. Rooted where he stood, the victim snorted." Okay, I give up. Which is the bull and which is the tree? Do bulls kill? Do trees snort? A metaphor is not a comparison. It's seeing one object (or person) as something else. "The ballerina was a swan gliding across the stage as if it were a glassy lake."

Adjectives and adverbs, used sparingly, <u>may</u> enhance your work, but do pay attention to <u>used sparingly</u>. Never use an adjective or adverb when a strong verb is available. "He walked quickly toward..." is neither as strong nor as vivid as "He hurried (or rushed, ran, raced) toward. . ." Of course, there are solid uses for adverbs and adjectives. Whenever the intended tone of dialogue needs clarification, an adverb does the job. ("Help me," she said <u>calmly</u>." Since <u>help me</u> is usually screamed, it needs clarification in this context.

As for adjectives, nothing says red like red, even if you have to enhance it with a similie to indicate which shade of red you're describing. There's nothing wrong with any particular adjective. What matters is the weakness your writing displays when you resort to them exclusively or use them abundantly.

One of the methods I use to avoid the temptation to overuse adjectives and adverbs works like this: Review your most recent work and highlight all adjectives and adverbs. Next, go though it again, testing for which can be replaced or made stronger by verbs, similies or metaphors. I think you'll like what you "see" when you've tried it.

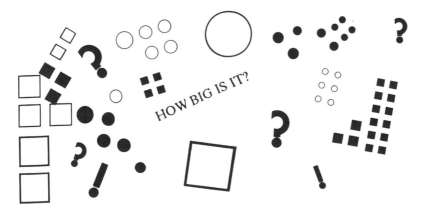

HOW BIG IS IT?

"No, this is not my new novel. It's my collection of rejections."

CONTESTANT

I'll write something special
I'll use the right slant
My words will be matchless
I won't say "I can't"

I'll spell check and proof
Each line, every clause
I won't watch the soaps
I won't even pause

As deadline draws closer
I write and re-write
It's got to be finished
By this Wednesday night

It's happened before
Though I hate to admit it
I've written my best
Too late to submit it

MAKES SENSE TO USE SENSES

We have five (5) senses: hearing, sight, touch, smell and taste. By incorporating these senses into your story, you make it not only more believable, but also more vivid and alive.

The following questions regarding each of our senses should help you become more aware of how they work in a story:

1) **SOUND.** What does the area sound like? Distant to close? What about the tone of voice? Pitch? Volume? What animal or mechanical sounds can be heard?

2) **SIGHT.** What does the protagonist see? What do the characters notice first? Colors? Shapes? Light? Dark?

3) **TOUCH.** What does the character feel? Skin? Cloth? Leather? Sand? Wet? Dry? Smooth? Rough? Show Character's reaction to what she touches or what touches her.

4) **SMELL.** Does the character notice smells? Are they pleasant? Unpleasant? Sharp? Faint? Acrid? Disgusting? Inspiring? Do odors trigger memory? Show reaction.

5) **TASTE.** What does the character like/hate to eat? Does air "taste" better in the spring? Does vomit burn tastebuds? Are kisses sweet? Tears

salty? What do emotions taste like? Show reactions.

It is easy to forget when the action is heavy, but an awareness of the senses we all use so automatically has to be consciously included in writing for the reader to get the feel of the character.

SAY WHAT?
(A WORD ABOUT DIALOGUE)

Make the "voice" of each character unique through your selection of phrasing and words. Don't have someone from New York saying "y'all" or "I'm fixin' to . . ."

Avoid unnecessary exchanges between characters. "Hello," and "How are you," are seldom necessary. Watch out for beginning dialogue with "Look," or "Well." We may speak that way, but it doesn't read well at all.

Do not use modifiers after said, unless the statement is ambiguous. Use "He shouted," not "He said loudly." Said is a perfectly acceptable attribution; however, by using a short action sentence prior to the character's speaking, attribution is often unnecessary. (Jane flopped onto the sofa. "I'm not going.") Who spoke and Jane's attitude are obvious.

Break up long rambling dialogue. It is difficult to read and slows the action.

Use dialogue to inform reader, but not "How is your mother, my dear sister whom I have not seen since I went away to Alaska to work on the pipeline twenty years ago." The other character surely knows his uncle and where he has been!

CHARTING YOUR PLOT

The Plot is how the story gets from A to Z. Basically, Who wants What and How they Get (or don't get) it, in spite of Who or What stands in their way.

A good plot hooks the reader right away, has real surprises and sub-plots connected to the primary story. A page-turner plot includes:

chapters that don't conclude;
intricate surprises;
escalating conflict;
strong emotion;
interesting context;
rich detailing;
satisfying conclusion.

Each chapter should be from three to twenty typed pages. Of course, like sentences and paragraphs, chapters shouldn't all be the same length. The length should depend on the turn of the story. It is easy to end a chapter before the next scene if the following scene is to be in another location or time. But if you wrap up all the loose ends before you move on, it is easy for the reader to put the book down. Try to end chapters with unanswered questions.

Intricate surprises stimulate the reader's imagination and keep her guessing.

Escalating conflict can be accomplished by having Character make choices that put her in a worse position. For instance, wanting desperately to make a good impression, she decides to take a bottle of expensive wine to her future mother-in-law when they meet for the first time, only to discover the woman is a recovered alcoholic.

Strong emotions need to be evoked in the reader. Make 'em laugh; make 'em cry. Make your characters so loved or hated that the reader is rooting (or booing) on every page.

Interesting context means that you are NOT telling the story of John Boring who gets up, goes to work, goes home, watches TV and goes to bed. If where and what happens to Character is vitally important to that character, it will likely be important to the reader.

Rich detailing adds flavor, texture and color to your story. Details can be overdone, like anything else. If you are describing a "greasy spoon" restaurant, one dirty dish is enough. Don't go on and on about dried egg on the fork, lipstick on the rim of the glass, something green stuck to the side of the plate. Move on to the condition of the floor, or the appearance of the people. Only include important details, those that add to the story.

In the end, the reader should react, be it with satisfaction that the villian got his due, the hero won after all or they lived happily ever after. You may want to let the villan get away, but most successful writers seem to conclude in a with satisfaction that reaffirms that virtue and hard work are rewarded.

MYSTERY OUTLINE

Be sure there's a body
By page one or two
Lead down the wrong alley
Come back with a clue
Unravel the motives
Keep stirring the stew
And make certain the guilty
Will suffer their due

NEW HACKER

Enter, Save, Edit, Copy
Move from here to there.
Could Hemingway or F. Scott
Do more with my software?

How I miss the sound of keys
Clacking as I write,
But my family's very grateful
To be sleeping through the night!

Know your market.

WRITERS READ WRITERS WHO WRITE TO BE READ

DON'T SIT ON A GOOD SETTING.
USE IT!

The setting or where the story takes place, includes time and location. It must be interesting--and **accurate**. Research is very important.

I once read the first page of a novel that started with ". . . hills sloping away from the gulf." It was set on the Texas Gulf Coast. I never read further. I have travelled most of the Texas Coast and never seen sloping hills. Do your homework! (That book was written by a man in New Jersey.)

Readers are more patient than screenviewers. If you let them learn about an area, they won't feel guilty for lounging around reading when they think they should be doing something "productive."

One way to make an opportunity to go into greater depth in the description of the setting is to have a character who has never been there. As Character sees everything for the first time, it will be as if the reader is there for the first time, too.

Be selective in application of your knowledge. You want to enhance your story, not write a travel piece. You do not need to use every bit of information you uncover.

Counterpoint in writing means the same thing it does in music: two parts going at once. For example, he wants to ask for divoice; they are in a restaurant where a pushy waiter interrupts dialogue.

In a setting, counterpoint is an unusual or interesting setting not usually associated with what is happening: closing a real estate transaction while trapped in an elevator; country girl stuck in city.

Time, also part of setting, is counterpoint when Character is in a shopping mall at three A.M. or a movie at noon or playground at night or an amusement park in the morning. I think you get the idea.

This idea can be overworked, like anything else, but does lend variety in setting and can build tension.

* * *

QUICKIE STORY FORMAT

HOOK

CHARACTER

DESIRE

OBSTACLE

CONFRONTATION

DECISION

CLIMAX

RESOLUTION

The longest book starts with one word.

FLASHBACKS and FORESHADOWING
(When and Why)

There is nothing wrong with flashbacks. There is something wrong with beginning a flashback too soon. Be sure your readers are hooked on the story and the characters first. Rarely, if ever, should a story be primarily a flashback.

Most stories are written in past tense. It has already happened. This is not the same as a flashback. In the story we say, "She ran." In a flashback, use, "She had run."

Flashbacks stop the forward motion of the story. It is usually more effective to spread background information throughout the story, revealing it in bits and pieces to escalate tension. Reveal the past through action and dialogue as much as possible.

Many times, the information we writers believe the readers must have is really information we need to understand the motivation of our characters. If background on Character is necessary, try to filter it in further over in the story by using action, dialogue or "memory triggers." (Character sees something that reminds him of the day she left.) Then you can glide into the parting scene. Or better yet, forget the parting scene and stick with the quick memory.

Foreshadowing (or Planting) is the bits of information that hint of what is to come. False foreshadowing is never welcomed by readers. They quickly feel cheated or duped and won't stand for it. Each detail must have a purpose. If something is mentioned more than once (especially in a mystery or suspense), it better mean something! Of course, planting a "red herring" is allowed.

GROWING AS A WRITER

As important as it is for writers to read, it is equally important for writers to know and learn from other writers. If you are not a member of a writers organization, find one and join. Volunteer for committees. Go to critique sessions. Ask questions. Listen. These other writers have been where you are and are always willing to help.

If you are afraid someone will "steal" your ideas, think of this: The ego of most writers is large enough that they would never try to pass off anything that came from someone else as their own creative efforts. Also, in the revised Copyright laws, anything you produce is automatically copyrighted by you when it is created.

In addition to mixing with other writers, I strongly recommend buying the annual **Writer's Market** and subscribing to the **Writer's Digest Magazine**. The continuing education provided in this literature will stimulate growth in any writer.

Another very helpful opportunity for writers is area conferences. Through writers' groups and the magazine, you can learn when these are scheduled and if the conference is also sponsoring writing contests. I would especially encourage you to enter local contests.

ALL TOLD

Writers' clubs and writers' news
Get my juices flowing,
But good outlines and characters
Tell me where I'm going.

You'd think it was the only book ever sold.

KID'S VIEWPOINT

Us kids are on the ceiling;
The dog has treed the cat.
Momma sits there typing,
Forgetting where she's at.
She's got more stories in her
Than Lego's got red blocks.
She hacks at that computer;
It takes some awful knocks.

Sometimes I hear her talking;
She's in her room alone.
I thought I'd never see her
Till I heard the phone.
She jerked the door wide open,
And come out on the run.
"It might be New York calling!"
We gathered for the fun.

Her face went pale. Her voice shook,
Then she let go with a whoop!
When she finally hung the phone up,
She swung me in a loop.
We squealed and danced around
Not really knowing why.
She said they'd really bought it,
Then she began to cry.

If other writing mothers go off their rockers, too,
It really is a puzzle. What's a kid to do?

TIP SHEET

1.   Keep a notebook.
          IDEAS
          PEOPLE
          PHRASES
          SETTINGS
          CLOTHES
          PEOPLE TAGS

2.   Write something every day. WRITERS WRITE!
          STORY
          POEM
          JOURNAL
          PAGE(S) IN YOUR NOVEL
          ARTICLE

3.   Get your work critiqued.
          WRITER'S GROUP
          TEACHER
          FRIEND (HONEST)
          MG/NWC/SCBW, etc.

4.   Polish, rewrite, polish, rewrite, polish and...

5.   Find a suitable market.
          WRITER'S MARKET
          LMP
          WRITER'S DIGEST
          THE WRITER
          NEWSLETTERS

6.   Select ten (10) places to send it; make labels for each. Send it to #1. When it comes back, send it to #2. When you run out of labels, rewrite and find 10 more places. Repeat until sold.

7.   Read, read, read!

IN YOUR GENRE
HOW-TO
THE CLASSICS

8.   Study the craft.
SEMINARS
CONFERENCES
CLASSES

WHETHER YOU WRITE WITH A. . .

OR A . . .

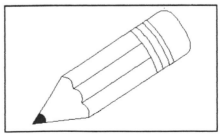

WRITE, WRITE AND RE-WRITE!

I AM A

~~RITER~~

~~WRIGHTER~~

~~WRITER~~

AUTHOR!

WHAT DO YOU DO?

When you're asked, "What do you do?" do you promptly say, "I'm a writer." If you don't, maybe you should.

No matter what your current means of financial support, if you are going to become a writer, you have to begin thinking of yourself as a writer. I know writers who support their writing addiction by working as doctors, engineers, secretaries, medical transcriptionists, professors, insurance salesmen, clerks, etc. I also know a few who care for children and home while trying to become writers. The ones who say they are writers, will have a greater chance of becoming writers than those who don't.

Your answer to the initial question forms your self-opinion. We are all motivated by how we think of ourselves. Try it. Say:

I AM A WRITER!

Each main character you develop has a self-opinion, too. It may well differ from the opinions held by other characters. Know this self-opinion, and you will know what motivates your character and how he will act and react in any situation.

A MOUTHFUL

A struggling writer plies her craft
To finish that wonderful first draft
Then after awhile she learns the truth
She's barely cut her very first tooth

THE WRONG WAY & THE <u>WRITE</u> WAY

Working on novels is very different from writing short pieces like this one or even short stories of three to five thousand words. A novel seems to go on forever. So far, I've completed two. One looking for a home; the other is sold (Walker & Co. for a '94 release). Now I'm working on my third. I love the characters, the setting, the plot. I like, actually, really and truly, like working on it. But that's not enough.

By nature, I'm multi-task orientated. I always have more projects in progress than an octopus could handle. Not that this is a bad way to be. Even some computers are into multi-tasking. Sounds important. What it is, however, is confusing. About the time I get another cartoon drawn, my muse comes up with a poem, or a short story, or this article or that... I've even got a board game in progress.

So what happens to my novels? They simmer. It took me six months to finish one. And two years to polish it. I could have written that many polished pages in four months if I'd stuck to one project. However, in the interim, I wrote and published two short stories, eight poems, six articles and self-published this book.

So, what is the right way to write? Any way you can. As much as you can. And what is the wrong way? Not writing at all. Writers write!

I can't write five pages a day on one project for very many days in a row. Once in a while, I wish I could. My brain is too full of other work. For me, it would be "wrong" to ignore my other projects and talents. For someone else, it would be "wrong" not to write straight through on one project before starting another.

If you're wondering if you're "doing it right" don't despair. If you're writing, you're doing it just fine!

...BUT REMEMBER---

FOLLOW THE ACTION...

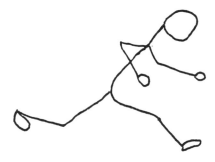

HALF-BAKED IDEAS

When a story hits my consciousness,
I think it is full grown;
But somewhere near the middle,
It takes off on its own.

VIEWPOINT
(WHOSE STORY IS IT?)

Point of View (POV) must be maintained in a story. It is very confusing for the reader to jump into and out of heads in the same scene. It just doesn't work.

For years, if a story was in more than one point of view, it was automatically rejected. With the prevelance of films that cut from character to character, switching points of view is more acceptable today. BUT, we still have to be diligent and stay in one head at a time.

One way to identify "where you are" is to check the verbs. John was content to . . . is in John's point of view. Being inside him is the only way to know if he was content. If you write John looked content to . . ., you are in another character's head.

Some stories need to take the reader into the antagonist's head. Make the change at a chapter break, or at the very least at the end of a scene by using an extra space to signify the change. That's acceptable.

Chapters changing to another character's viewpoint sometimes feel like "Meanwhile, back at the ranch." The change should be necessary--or omitted.

* * *

LYNN'S LIMERICK

There once was a writer named Lynn
Who thought every word she would pen
Should be deathless prose
'Cause everyone knows
It's so hard to re-write again

A TO Z ON POV

How clear can you see
Your character's POV?
If it swings to and fro
No agent can know
Whose story you tell.
It never will sell.
Rework it again,
Beginning to end.
Each scene, every sequel,
All things being equal,
Must show through his eyes,
From feelings to skies.

If you're still not sure
Please, play it demure
And gently refer to
"He thought" and "He knew."
Throw in a few clauses:
"He guessed at the causes,:
Say "Something reminds him. . ."
Or what he will do when. . .
These quick little tips,
So fresh from my lips,
Will help all to see
Your strong POV.

RECOMMENDED ADDITIONS TO YOUR LIBRARY
The following list is compiled in the order I read them.

TECHNIQUES OF A SELLING WRITER
Dwight V. Swain
University of Oklahoma Press
1005 Asp Avenue
Norman, OK 73019-0445

CREATING CHARACTERS:
HOW TO BUILD STORY PEOPLE
Dwight V. Swain
Writer's Digest Books
1507 Dana Avenue
Cincinnati, OH 45207

FROM PRINTOUT TO PUBLISHED
Michael Seidman
Carroll & Graf Publishers, Inc.
260 Fifth Avenue
New York, NY 10001

SPIDER, SPIN ME A WEB:
Lawrence Block on Writing Fiction
Writer's Digest Books
(see above)

LIVING THE DREAM
Michael Seidman
Carroll & Graf Publishers

WRITING NOVELS THAT SELL
Jack M. Bickham
Simon & Schuster Fireside Imprint
1230 Avenue of the Americas
New York, NY 10020

DIALOGUE IS <u>NOT</u> CONVERSATION!

Dialogue is not the same as conversation. The more you try to make it sound like an everyday verbal exchange, the more you weaken your dialogue.

Keep dialogue short, organized, to the point, focused. It should advance the story and be controlled.

Each character must speak in his own voice. Characters should not sound like each other. Know your character and you will know his voice. Is the character country? Educated? Vulgar? Prim? Use phrasing and word choice accordingly.

Too much dialogue can become difficult to read. About 50/50 between dialogue and narration "reads" well.

Listen. Keep an observation journal of phrases, style and pet comments. Keep tone of characters consistent.

STRUCTURE

A screenplay as well as a novel can be broken into sections: setup of characters, development of conflict, all is lost, climax and ending.

A screenplay is divided into three acts, just like a stage play; however, a screenplay is labeled in four parts. These are called Act I, Act IIA, Act IIB and Act III. Each section is approximately one quarter of the total. In a novel, this would mean each section would run from about 75 to 150 pages, depending on the depth of the novel. In a screenplay, each is 30 pages or about 30 minutes.

Each Act has a distinct purpose in furthering the story.

ACT I - Introduce characters, in character with tags. Introduce the story world; setting, time, etc. Set drama. Make characters and world special. We all live in the real world. When we see a movie or read a novel, we want something that takes us away from our own world. Develop the fictional dream. Also, include any necessary backstory (background)--the things the reader needs to know to believe this story is "in progress."

Strongly establish the central character (protagonist). Let the audience or reader know who the story is about. Give him special focus through language, attitude, costume, etc. Others talking behind his back about his patience, loneliness, temper is one way to do this.

The central character needs to have an emotional reason for his decisions besides a logical one or instead of a logical one. Readers want to see an intense and driven character.

REMEMBER--the central character is the decision maker, the one we follow throughout the story.

ACT I can also be broken into:

1) Establish central character.

2) Identify premise. What is the story about? What is the theme? This can be worked into dialogue. If it can be summed up in one sentence, let someone say it.

3) Establish circumstances. Paint the character's world. Is it dreary? Bright? Sci-fi? History? City? Country?

PLOT POINT

Near the end of Act I, there should be a huge event that throws the central character for a loop--changes the status of his world. This is "Turning Point 1."

ACT IIA

Act IIA is where characters are enriched. This section should show a lot of effort, ups and downs toward established goal. It can also be a good place for a "sit down" scene where one character tells another the how and why of it all--while they wait for something awful or exciting that may not come off. This section is often used for a bonding moment, central character to another, i.e., recognizes true love, shows strong attachment to someone or something as a result of what has happened.

The turning point near the end of this section is called MID-POINT. It is often the first Turning Point to the B-story. (B-story involves the secondary characters and their problems, but is connected to A-story.) Whatever happens in B-story should color the rest of A-story. The adventure keeps going, but because of B-story, more is at stake. It adds a HEAVY COMPLICATION.

ACT IIB

Here, the adventure keeps pumping; there are more problems to overcome. This should be the part where our hero experiences ALL IS LOST and makes a DECISION near the end of this section that is called TURNING POINT 2.

ACT III

This is where push comes to shove and our central character either wins or loses. He lays it all on the line. It is important that something that means everything to him is at stake; love, money or prestige. The story should have a HIGH CLIMAX that proves perseverance, honesty, truth, love, et al, win again. This is why we read, why we go to movies: to verify that justice prevails!

CHECK IT OUT

We all need some way to be sure we've covered all the bases. One of my favorite ways to check out the storyline is with the following format:

(title) is the story of (tag or identification, i.e., lawyer, photographer) (central character's name), who because of (burning desire) decides to (what) resulting in (problem) and (problem) leading to (all is lost). But, because of (magic moment), Protagonist decides to (final confrontation) resulting in (victory or defeat).

This keeps me on track. It is also a mini-format for a synopsis.

WHEN PIGS FLY

I never knew a pig could fly
Nor that a sheep could soar.
I sometimes think they'll fill the sky
When my book's in the store.

I finished it three years ago,
And sent that bundle packing.
An editor and publisher
Are all that I am lacking.

SOOTHING LIFE

Write it, then edit.
Tighten it here;
Chop off the extras,
No matter how dear.

Double space, margins,
Spell-check every page,
But when it comes back,
Don't fret, fume or rage.

Re-package, re-stamp it;
Keep manuscripts moving.
Relax and enjoy
This life that's so soothing.

THE CHOICE IS YOURS--OR IS IT?

It is my belief that anyone with a strong desire--a compulsion--to write, also has the raw talent to write. I have learned that no matter how great the talent, without developing the craft, a writer is only a scribbler.

TIPS covers only a fragment of the information needed to develop the craft of writing. There is so much more. Read the works of Dwight Swain, Jack Bickham and others.

Most of us write because we have to. It's a blessing and a curse. Most days we wouldn't trade writing for all the coffee in Brazil. When we're re-writing and marketing, we'd probably trade for one coffee bean.

If you still have a choice about writing, it's not too late to escape. Throw yourself into community service until you don't have a spare moment to write. If it's too late and you're hooked, you have only one choice: write, write, re-write, re-write, re-write, THEN SEND IT OUT! It will never find a home sitting in a drawer or stacked on a shelf.

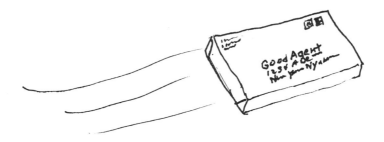

FOLLOW THE ACTION

FIRST: The beginning of your book sets the tone for the rest of the story, introduces the central characters and blocks out the conflict. It should have a lurking sense of danger. Terrible trouble, collision course, life is changing. I should be building in intensity, but don't beat a catalyst to death! Hook the reader early. In a romance, the couple meets early; in a mystery, the murder happens early; in a mainstream, the problem is established early. Reveal conflict with dialogue. Give the reader only enough information to follow the story. Limit number of characters. Every story must have a sense of urgency. Establish it early. Every action must be related to the central conflict, including the subplots.

SECOND: The middle is for tightening the noose, escalating the tension, revealing pertinent information, adding to the problems, raising the stakes. Delay is not tension. Hurdles that make the situation worse work better. Coincidence is not good. The reader feels the author's hand and the fictional dream is broken. The only time coincidence is useful is when it makes matters worse. The last complication is always the worst complication. The big gloom. All is lost!

THIRD: The end is for the triumph of human spirit over adversity as a result of decision and perseverance. Once the climax (solution) is reached, wrap up all loose ends quickly. Do not leave subplots (B-story) unresolved.

* * *

Make your readers laugh or cry, but never indifferent.

CRITIQUE OR CRITIC?

Having your manuscript critiqued by other writers is a major help in seeing your work through someone else's eyes. In most writers groups time is set aside for reading and critiquing. These groups are operated in various ways. Some writers insist on every member of the group having a copy of what is being read. Others don't seem to object to trying to follow only oral presentations. Since we are writers, it seems to me that how a story reads is as important, if not more so, than how it sounds.

Critiquing is not giving opinions on the subject--only on the writing. In other words, someone who doesn't like football should still be able to critique a story on football. It should be the quality of the writing that is evaluated, not the subject.

A good critique always points out the strong points of the piece. We all need reinforcement of our efforts. The problem areas, or weak points should be specific. Is the piece vivid? Does it evoke emotions? Is it focused? Is the dialogue interesting? Does it move the plot? Does the description have a purpose? Is there interesting conflict? Is the plot believable or contrived? How can it be improved?

When you get involved in a critique group, try to be helpful. It is not helpful to say you like or don't like a story. Listen closely to the use of adjectives and adverbs. Could the writer have used more powerful verbs? Does it sing-song from lack of sentence variety?

I have learned as much about my own writing from listening to other writers' work being critiqued as I have when my work is in the spotlight.

MARKETING

There is an old saw in the sales business that "nothing happens 'til somebody sells something."

If you're writing strictly for your own enjoyment, there's certainly nothing wrong with that. But if you want to become a selling writer, you have to learn how to market your work.

One of the basics of marketing is the right resources. Begin with Writer's Market. This book is published annually and can be bought at most book stores or ordered through Writer's Digest Magazine. (If you're not familiar with this magazine, you should be.) In Writer's Market there are listings of book publishers, agents and magazines, along with a hefty amount of quality information on how to prepare your manuscript.

Another, weightier tome is Literary Market Place. A good deal more expensive, it is carried by all libraries. It's a resource volume, so take plenty of notepaper with you to copy the names and addresses of publishers and agents that sound as if they would be receptive to your type of work.

Most agents and publishers prefer that you send work to only one agent or publisher at a time. Most writers use the shotgun approach. It is considered courteous to inform the recipient of your manuscript if it is a multiple submission.

When submitting a book length manuscript to an agent or publisher, never send the complete manuscript. And never, never send your only copy! And always always send an SASE (self-addressed stamped envelope) with sufficient postage for the return of your manuscript. I always include a reply postcard, too. The front of the card has the correct postage and MY address. The back has "Date Rec'd:" and "Expect reply by:" with the title and my byline at the top. I find this most helpful in keeping track of where I've sent what and when I can expect to hear something.

Instead of the complete manuscript, send a cover letter and the first three chapters (up to 50 pages), and a synopsis. Writer's Market explains what goes into a cover letter and also goes into greater detail on the above. The magazine keeps me current on changes in the marketplace. As you can see, I strongly recommend them. (Too bad I don't get a commission from them.)

Now about rejections--you'll get 'em. Every writer gets rejection slips. Sometimes it's timing, sometimes it's selecting the wrong publisher or agent. Everything is specialized to some extent. A publisher who produces only textbooks isn't going to read your historical romance. **Know your market.**

* * *

WRITE WHAT YOU KNOW

Write settings you know. Write characters you know. (Combine parts of different people.) But write about the feelings you've experienced.

What you know is that every feeling has an outward manifestation. Show the reader these symptoms of the character's feelings. You know how feelings feel. You may not have had a lover spurn you, but as a child did you ever have a pet die? The feeling of loss is equally intense. Show that feeling.

SYNOPSIS SINS & SOLUTIONS

When you're thumbing through the market guides for a place to send your fiction manuscript, you'll notice most listings say, "Submit outline/synopsis and sample chapters". While some editors do want a chapter-by-chapter outline of a fiction manuscript, more often they want a five to seven page synopsis, but prefer a detailed outline of a proposed nonfiction work; hence the slash. Since we're discussing fiction and from this chapter title you hope this is going to be about how to write a synopsis, I won't go into outlining.

The ultimate sin for a writer is to waste prime writing time unnecessarily depleting mental energy. For too long I committed this sin by wasting my time and the unfortunate editor's who received my overdone submissions. It's with this in mind that I conclude it is a sin to send both outline and synopsis.

A second, and possibly worse sin is refusing to disclose the ending of a story. Although it seems like a sure-fire way to get an editor to request the rest of your gripping manuscript, nothing short of handwritten prose could get you a quicker rejection. No one has to guess about your inexperience or ignorance when you leave out the ending. In effect you are saying, "I hope I'm a writer, but I don't want to be bothered with learning anything about marketing."

Marketing is 50% of writing. Withholding the ending was one of my early, childish ploys that said, "nah-na-nah. If you want to know how it ends, you'll have to read it a-a-all."

Editors don't play games.

A third sinful waste of time and energy is to tell it all. When you list every character, every scene change, you only confuse yourself and the editor. It is the essence, the flow, the story they want. The details, the quality of the characterizations, the ability to show instead of tell, should be evident in the sample chapters you include.

Now that you know the three major sins to avoid when writing a synopsis, you should have no trouble whipping out a perfect synopsis. Do keep in mind, please, that this is only one writer's sin list. With effort I'm not willing to expend, I could probably disclose several more. (I can only stand so much confession at one time.) If you asked editors I've dealt with, they could most likely extend the list ad infinitum.

The same possibilities for expansion are also true for solutions. For every five writers there are at least ten ways to handle a synopsis. So far, this way has worked well for me.

First of all, my synopsis is always in present tense, no matter what tense the book is in. After a "hook" like. . .

"Photographer Alyson Tidwell got more than she bargained for when she bought Trey's house in the Montrose section of Houston."

I then use the following outline:

1) First paragraph--possible opening sentence: (Title) is the story of (main character) who (goal), but (conflict or what stands in his/her way).

2) In approximately one to one and one half pages, contrast the protagonist and antagonist as they are at the opening of the book.

3)   Topic sentence for second paragraph, suggested only: The story opens with (main character) trying to (desire), in spite of (obstacle or conflict).

4)   Generate questions; show problems--both emotional and physical. Answers are not necessary at this point. This should complete page two.

5)   In the next three to five pages, describe what happens-- in present tense. Tell exactly how the protagonist and antagonist come into conflict. Show how the protagonist's solutions cause further problems.

6)   Devote one paragraph to each subplot. Possibly: While (protagonist) is. . ., (whoever) is. . ..

7)   Tell clearly and precisely how the primary conflict is resolved. **Do not hide the ending.**

8)   Present your synopsis double-spaced in clean crisp type on 8 1/2" X 11" 20# nonerasable white bond paper.

And there you have it. Eight simple steps for a sin-free synopsis. Using this guide helps me summarize my work instead of interpreting its theme.

While no one can guarantee any formula for getting an agent or editor to read your manuscript, a well-written synopsis can open the door.

□ □ □

WHO CARES?

When it comes to your characters, if you don't care about them, neither will the reader.

One of the wonderful benefits of reading is having our emotions manipulated. With a well-written story, we can experience the variety of feelings many of us are denied in our everyday world. We feel the panic of a trapped hero, the rush of the heroine's blush, the fear of a near-victim, the jubilance of the victorious. As writers, one feeling we do not want a reader to have toward our characters is apathy.

We want our characters to be immediately loved or hated. Cheered or booed.

If we don't write with emotion for our characters, it is not likely we will draw the emotions we are trying to elicit from readers.

Build characters, or take them from bits of people you know, but create characters you feel strongly about--characters you love to love and love to hate. Passion. Your passion for your characters will show.

FROM THE AUTHOR

I hope reading this little book has helped you as much as writing it has helped me. If you would like additional copies of TIPS FOR BEGINNING FICTION WRITERS, send $10 in check or money order to:

Talent by the Lb
P O Box 531
Sugar Land TX 77487-0531

* * * * * *

A very special thanks to
Dot Fowler,
my editor and my friend.

* * * * * *

ABOUT THE AUTHOR

Lynn Bradley is the author of STAND-IN FOR MURDER, a 1994 release from Walker & Company. She is also an internationally published, award winning writer of fiction, nonfiction and poetry. Like her writing, her cartoons and illustrations have appeared in literary journals, magazines and newspapers. (The foregoing is called literary license. I had one article in a Canadian publication, I won a couple of local contests, but I really did write a book that was accepted by Walker & Company.) She lives with her husband Bob in Richmond, Texas.

Mom! Did you tell Santa all we wanted was your book published!